• I Can •
Smile

Sarah Levete

Aladdin/Watts
London • Sydney

© Aladdin Books Ltd 2002

Designed and produced by
Aladdin Books Ltd
28 Percy Street
London W1T 2BZ

First published in
Great Britain in 2002 by
Franklin Watts
96 Leonard Street
London EC2A 4XD

ISBN 0 7496 4471 0
A catalogue record for this book is
available from the British Library.

Editor
Jim Pipe

Literacy Consultant
Jackie Holderness
Westminster Institute of Education,
Oxford Brookes University

Design
Flick, Book Design and Graphics

Illustration
Mary Lonsdale for SGA

The author, Sarah Levete, has written
several books for young people
on social and personal issues.

The consultant, Dr. Donna Pincus, Ph.D., is a Research
Assistant Professor and the Director of the Child and Adolescent
Fear and Anxiety Treatment Program at Boston University, USA.

Contents

Welcome!

It is great to be full of smiles and laughs, but at times you may feel like crying, throwing things or even hitting out.

This book helps you to accept and understand your feelings – even the not so good ones. Then it's easier to smile again.

From feeling cross to feeling bored, this book looks at ways to get back to feeling happy and calm again.

Read on and find out how to deal with lots of different situations, like the death of someone you love or bullying at school.

About This Book

In every chapter, there are stories about children like you. Look out for the coloured boxes.

Each story has a different colour. Find out how each person deals with the same things that may upset you.

Every chapter also gives examples of other feelings and situations that make people feel unsure.

At the end of each chapter find out how the people in the stories cope with their feelings.

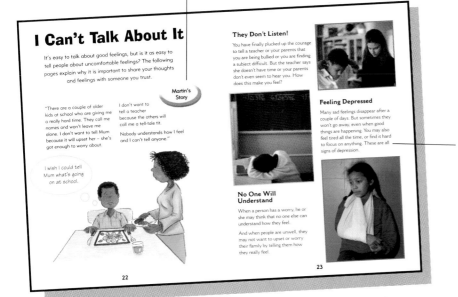

Learn ways to deal with difficult feelings or situations.

Turn to the back for tips on how to feel happier and for lists of helpful books, websites and addresses.

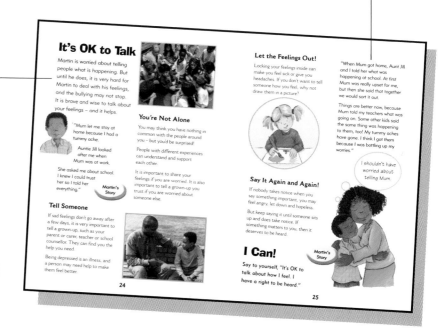

How Do I Feel?

When you woke up this morning, how did you feel – happy, grumpy or serious? How do you feel now? Read on and find out why it's important to understand and accept all your feelings.

Zoe promised to sit next to me. What should I do?

Bella's Story

"I was so excited about the school trip to the theatre. But it was the worst day ever! My best friend, Zoe, sat next to another girl on the coach! She totally ignored me for the whole journey. I didn't want anyone to see I was upset, so I pretended not to mind. At the theatre, Zoe sat right behind me but still didn't say a thing. I was so upset I felt sick and I couldn't enjoy the show."

What Do You Feel?

Would you be quiet like Bella if you were upset? Or would you get loud and angry? The words on the list below describe some of the things people feel when they are upset. Do you find some emotions hard to explain?

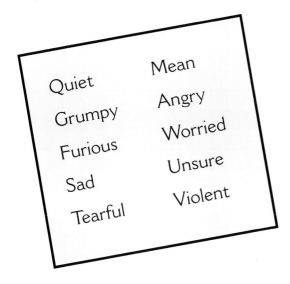

Quiet
Grumpy
Furious
Sad
Tearful
Mean
Angry
Worried
Unsure
Violent

Happy or Sad?

Look at the two photos below. How do you think the children feel?

A person's face tells us a lot about his or her mood. But be careful – do tears always mean that someone is sad?

Ouch!

How does it feel when you do a cool stunt on your skateboard or skip really fast in front of your friends?

How does it feel if you fall and graze your knee? Does it also hurt because you think people will laugh at you?

I Feel...

Bella is upset but pretends to feel OK. But her feelings won't go away until she accepts and admits that she feels hurt and upset. Then the upset feelings will soon pass.

Bella's Story

"By the time I got home, my head was spinning.

As soon as I saw Mum, I burst into tears and told her how I really felt. It was such a relief!"

Different Reactions

Everyone reacts differently. After falling over, some people just get up and carry on. Others can feel upset or embarrassed and run off.

If the way you react annoys you, it can help to think about why you react the way you do.

What Are Tears For?

Tears show how you feel inside. They let you show your emotions and help you to let go of your feelings.

But tears don't only show sadness. People often cry at happy times such as a grandparent's birthday party.

They also cry with relief after an event they were worried about, such as finishing an important race.

8

Words and Pictures

Describing your emotions helps you to understand and accept what you are feeling. It makes it easier for others to understand you as well!

Try to use words that describe clearly how you feel – do you feel a little bit anxious, or sick with worry?

It can help to write a story or a poem about the way you feel.

I Can!

Say to yourself: "I can accept how I feel". Then the feelings will pass.

I'm really glad we're still friends, Zoe!

"When I tried to hide my feelings at the show, it made a big knot in my stomach. It felt much better after I had a good cry and talked to Mum.

Bella's Story

Mum said it is important to accept feelings. She said you shouldn't push them down, because they just keep popping up! Instead, you should try to notice them the way you would a colour. Once you get your emotions out in the open, it's easier to deal with them.

Zoe rang later. I told her how I felt and she apologised for ignoring me."

Things Change

Sometimes upsetting things happen, but you can't change them. Perhaps your pet dies or your parents split up. Read on and find out how people cope when their feelings are turned upside-down.

Kia's Story

"Granny died last week. I can't stop crying because I miss her so much and because I know she won't come back. She was lovely and made us all feel so happy.

But my brother Leo acts as if nothing has happened.

He's also a lot more grumpy than usual.

Maybe he didn't really care about Gran. He doesn't even want to talk about her."

I miss Gran. Leo is so mean he doesn't even care.

Can I Change It Back?

When parents split up, it is a grown-up decision that children can't change, however much they may want to.

Some children feel very lonely, missing one parent very much. Others are angry or pretend not to care, even though they feel upset inside.

Will I Always Feel Sad?

When something very upsetting happens, such as when a family breaks up or your favourite pet dies, you may cry so much that you may worry you won't be able to stop.

You may go to sleep feeling miserable and wake up sad because you can't change what has happened.

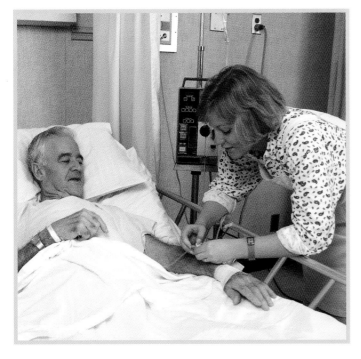

I Can't Face It

Kia is angry because Leo doesn't react like her. But everyone gets upset in their own way.

Perhaps someone you really care about has to go to hospital because they are very ill. But even though you are very upset, you may not want to see the person unwell or in hospital.

Feelings Pass

People react to unhappy situations in different ways. Some feel better quickly. Others take longer – and that's OK, too.

Kia's Story

"Gran wouldn't want me to cry forever. There's nothing wrong with crying, but I want to start going out with my friends again. Having fun doesn't mean I didn't care about Gran.

I think Leo is upset inside. He's always up in his bedroom alone. Perhaps I should go and cheer him up."

Moving On

The feelings you have won't disappear straight away after a big change, such as your parents splitting up or losing a pet.

There is no need to push the feelings away or ignore them. You have a right to feel the way you do. In time, the feelings will pass.

When you feel ready, do the things you enjoy. A game with a friend or a a good film can help you smile again, even if just for a short while.

Ways to Show You Care

If you are too upset to see a friend or family member who is ill, are there other ways to show you care?

Sending a card that you have written or drawn, or speaking on the telephone shows someone you care. It will make you feel better, too.

Get well soon love tom xxx

Everyone Cries!

Some people think it's babyish or silly to cry. It's not. Everyone cries, even grown-ups like mums, dads and teachers. If you feel awkward crying in front of friends, try to find somewhere private.

After a good cry, you may still feel sad but you'll feel calmer because crying releases the feelings inside. And remember, the tears will stop!

I Can!

I can't change what's happened but in time I can smile again.

"Even though I thought I'd never stop crying about Gran, I did! I still miss her and sometimes feel sad when I look at her photograph. But I laugh when I think about the fun we had together.

I've moved up a year at school and have some great new friends. Leo is less grumpy now and we've started to talk about all the happy times Gran gave us."

Kia's Story

Gran would be pleased to see me having fun.

I'm In A Grump!

Have you ever wanted to stamp your feet, shout at people or throw your toys around? You're probably feeling grumpy! Everyone feels grumpy from time to time, for lots of different reasons.

"Dad wouldn't let me go to my friend Ben's party because he wanted me to go to my cousin's house instead.

How mean is that? Ben's party would have been really cool. I was so angry, I shouted at Dad.

Then I slammed my bedroom door and refused to come out.

I was boiling with anger inside. I even tore up my party invite from Ben."

Ade's Story

I hate you for making me miss Ben's party.

Feeling Mad

Sometimes people make us cross, but things can make us angry, too. It can be tricky trying to fix a broken bike or play a difficult card game! Some people become so annoyed or frustrated that they end up in a bad mood.

And it's even harder to do something when you're in a grump!

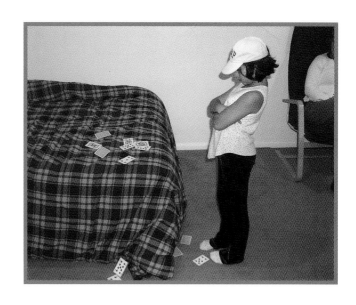

Quick or Slow?

It's often little things that can quickly change a person's mood. Missing a shot in a game or not being allowed something you want can make you furious.

Grumpy feelings also build up slowly. It may be something unimportant that finally makes you blow your top.

That's Not Fair!

Can you remember someone saying something nasty to you or spoiling your game just because they were in a bad mood?

Grumpy people try to turn everyone else grumpy as well. It's very unfair!

Calming Down

It can be hard to shake off a grumpy mood! But these pages give you some tips for getting rid of cross feelings.

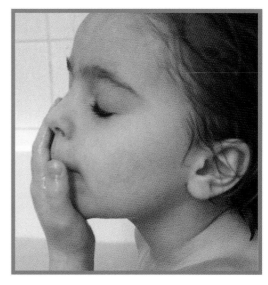

"I sulked in my room for ages. I wanted to calm down but every time I thought about Ben's party, I felt mad again.

Then I remembered what my brother always says, 'If you feel upset, do something'!"

Ade's Story

Try This!

Actions help! Here are some safe things to try:

- Splash your face with water
- Take some slow deep breaths
- Shout loudly in front of the mirror
- Punch a pillow.

When you feel angry, have a go!

What's Up?

Knowing why you feel grumpy helps you get rid of cross feelings.

Do you find it hard to share games or wait for your turn? Remember your turn will come.

Do you want everything to be perfect? Or do you hate losing? Accept that things don't always work out the way you want.

Are you grumpy in order to get your own way? It won't always work – and it's upsetting for others.

Is there another problem troubling you? Try talking to someone you trust. You'll feel better – and less grumpy!

Take Five

Have you ever tried these quick ways of calming down?

• Walk away from a stormy situation
• Count to five, ten or twenty
• Imagine you are on a sunny beach, playing in the sea, and nothing matters
• Think of something funny

Can you think of other things you can do?

What a shot! I feel better already!

I Can!

Think: "I can throw my grumpy feelings in the bin, and choose some nicer ones instead".

Ade's Story

"I went out and kicked a football around. I soon forgot about being mad – I was having more fun playing.

When I got home, I said sorry to Dad for being so grumpy. In fact, I had a good time at my cousin's.

Ben also rang up and invited me to his house next weekend to play with his new games. Cool!"

Feeling Down

Have you ever woken up with a glum feeling? Do you ever feel you have lost your smile and can't get it back again? Read on and you'll find out how to make yourself feel happy again!

Kim's Story

Usually I love this class, but today it's just boring me.

"I feel really low today. I just don't seem interested in anything and can't be bothered to make the effort. I don't even want to go out with my friends after school.

My friends think I am being unfriendly. But it's just because I feel really fed up.

What upsets me most is that I don't know why I feel like this."

Feeling Unwell

With an earache or an upset tummy, you can't do the things that you usually do. Even if you're longing to play outside or go to a friend's house, your parents or carer will probably say "No!".

This can be frustrating and you may end up feeling fed up and annoyed, as well as sick!

Difficulties at Home

Difficult times at home can make you feel miserable. It may be parents arguing or worrying about money, or a brother or sister in trouble.

This can make it hard to enjoy games or laugh at the funniest jokes. You may only be able to think of what's happening at home.

I'm Bored!

Nothing to do? Nowhere to go? No one to play with?

Feeling bored or restless can upset you.

You may snap at people in your family, or get fed up with even your favourite toys and games.

Smiling Again!

Give your feelings a holiday! For a while, do something a bit different. You may feel better afterwards!

Kim's Story

"Dad knew something was wrong when I wouldn't eat my favourite meal. I told him I felt down in the dumps. He said everyone feels fed up sometimes.

Dad suggested I read a good book to take my mind off things. I'll try the one that my friend keeps raving about."

Do Something New!

It's no fun feeling bored but it's easy to get rid of the feeling!

Make the things around you more interesting – use them in a new way. That cupboard could become a castle! Make plans to join a new club or start a new hobby, such as flying kites.

Have a Laugh

It can seem unfair when you can't do the things that other people do. But feeling unhappy won't change the situation. Sharing a smile or a giggle can make you feel much better!

If you can't go out, play a game or do a puzzle. Ask for a book of jokes from the library and learn the best ones so you can tell them to your friends.

I Can!

It's natural to feel low sometimes. It helps to talk about it, but it is also good to do something active or new to take your mind off things.

Look after Yourself

Even if your mum, dad or best friend has problems, don't forget to take care of yourself. Eat well and have plenty of sleep – it's easier to cope when you are fit and healthy.

If problems at home become too upsetting, talk to a grown-up you trust outside your family.

If you know people who are having a hard time, make a special effort to include them in your games.

"This book is brilliant!

It's such a good story. When I was reading it, I forgot about feeling sad and fed up.

I had a really good sleep and woke up feeling a bit brighter. I'm going to go round to my friend's house after school today.

Kim's Story

There's a new book coming out by the same author – I can't wait!

Dad said if I ever feel like that again, it's important to tell him if the sad feelings don't go away. "

I'm so glad I told Dad how I felt.

I Can't Talk About It

It's easy to talk about good feelings, but is it as easy to tell people about uncomfortable feelings? The following pages explain why it is important to share your thoughts and feelings with someone you trust.

Martin's Story

"There are a couple of older kids at school who are giving me a really hard time. They call me names and won't leave me alone. I don't want to tell Mum because it will upset her – she's got enough to worry about.

I don't want to tell a teacher because the others will call me a tell-tale tit.

Nobody understands how I feel and I can't tell anyone."

I wish I could tell Mum what's going on at school.

They Don't Listen!

You have finally plucked up the courage to tell a teacher or your parents that you are being bullied or you are finding a subject difficult. But the teacher says she doesn't have time or your parents don't even seem to hear you. How does this make you feel?

No One Will Understand

When a person has a worry, he or she may think that no one else can understand how they feel.

And when people are unwell, they may not want to upset or worry their family by telling them how they really feel.

Feeling Depressed

Many sad feelings disappear after a couple of days. But sometimes they won't go away, even when good things are happening. You may also feel tired all the time, or find it hard to focus on anything. These are all signs of depression.

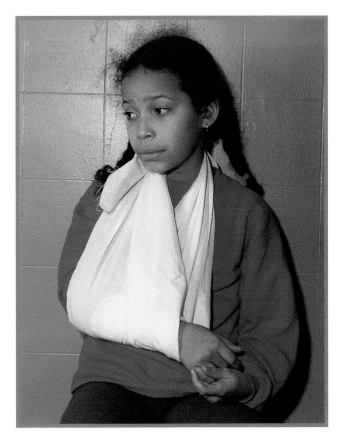

It's OK to Talk

Martin is worried about telling people what is happening. But until he does, it is very hard for Martin to deal with his feelings, and the bullying may not stop. It is brave and wise to talk about your feelings – and it helps.

You're Not Alone

You may think you have nothing in common with the people around you – but you'd be surprised!

People with different experiences can understand and support each other.

It is important to share your feelings if you are worried. It is also important to tell a grown-up you trust if you are worried about someone else.

"Mum let me stay at home because I had a tummy ache.

Auntie Jill looked after me when Mum was at work.

She asked me about school. I knew I could trust her so I told her everything."

Martin's Story

Tell Someone

If sad feelings don't go away after a few days, it is very important to tell a grown-up, such as your parent or carer, teacher or school counsellor. They can find you the help you need.

Being depressed is an illness, and a person may need help to make them feel better.

Let the Feelings Out!

Locking your feelings inside can make you feel sick or give you headaches. If you don't want to tell someone how you feel, why not draw them in a picture?

Say It Again and Again!

If nobody takes notice when you say something important, you may feel angry, let down and hopeless.

But keep saying it until someone sits up and does take notice. If something matters to you, then it deserves to be heard.

I Can!

Say to yourself, "It's OK to talk about how I feel. I have a right to be heard."

"When Mum got home, Aunt Jill and I told her what was happening at school. At first Mum was really upset for me, but then she said that together we would sort it out.

Things are better now, because Mum told my teachers what was going on. Some other kids said the same thing was happening to them, too! My tummy aches have gone. I think I got them because I was bottling up my worries."

I shouldn't have worried about telling Mum.

Martin's Story

Ups And Downs

There are days when you feel great and days when you feel not so great! It happens to everyone! Feelings come and feelings go – that's what makes life interesting.

Kate was buzzing when she came home. Now she's miserable.

"My sister Kate is so up and down. When she's at home whatever you say can put her in a mood. She's always complaining that it's so boring at home.

Nothing Mum does or I do makes any difference. We can't make her smile. I find it really upsetting sometimes."

Harry's Story

Like A Yo Yo

Some people seem to be either very happy or very low – with no in-between. They swing like a yo yo from feeling super happy to super gloomy.

It's quite confusing to be around someone who is up and down like this from one moment to the next.

Can't Stop Laughing!

Have you ever had an attack of the giggles? Your tummy might start to ache because you are laughing so much!

Then your friends start to laugh – and none of you can stop!

Changing Moods

Some people love lots of noise and may feel frustrated and moody in quieter places. Others like things to be peaceful and become grumpy when things are too noisy.

Perhaps you know someone who gets grumpy when they are hungry or tired?

I'm Really OK!

Harry is upset by Kate's moods. Kate needs to find a way of feeling more content and less up and down. But Harry also needs to do his own thing when Kate is in a mood.

Harry's Story

"Mum took me shopping and we bought Kate some clay and a book on pottery for her birthday. Now she is really into it, making bowls and plates!

I've decided that if Kate is moody, I'm just going to get on with my own stuff. It doesn't help anyone if I get upset and moody, too."

Keeping Balanced

We all have ups and downs, good days and bad days. Our feelings change but we need to balance them. Remember who you are inside and that whatever you feel, you are still the same person.

When you feel low, think of the good times and try to smile inside. Remember – actions help!

If you feel as if you will burst with excitement, take a couple of deep breaths to relax you. Then you can enjoy what you're doing without bursting!

That's Life!

All through your life, even when you're as old as your grandparents, you will go through lots of different feelings. Some feelings are good and others not so good.

Remember that sad feelings pass and can change. Life is full of wonderful surprises that can make us feel good.

Enjoy It

Happy times are special – enjoy them. Being happy is a wonderful feeling!

When you feel happy, share your smile. Do you know anyone with a friendly smile who likes to make others happy?

I Can!

I can smile *and* I can cry. It's OK!

Kate is much nicer to be around. She smiles more now!

"Kate's easier to get on with now. She's realised that quiet times aren't all bad! I think she thought she had to have fun the whole time and was grumpy because she couldn't be out with her friends all the time.

Harry's Story

I'm doing more of the things I enjoy, instead of worrying about Kate. I feel happier, too."

Remember

When you feel sad or upset, try to think of these tips. They can help you feel better.

• Just telling someone how you feel can make a worry seem much less upsetting.

• Talk to friends, family and teachers – that's what they are there for!

• It's easier to cope with things that upset you if you look after yourself. Remember to eat well and have plenty of sleep.

• Sad feelings pass and can change. Life is full of wonderful things and surprises that can make you feel better.

• Everyone has ups and downs, highs and lows, and good and bad days.

• If you are feeling sad, give your feelings a holiday! For a while, do something a bit different. Play with a friend or try a new hobby.

• If something makes you feel grumpy, a few deep breaths can really calm you down. Splashing water on your face helps, too, or try to think of something that makes you laugh.

Read About It

You can also look in your library or bookshop for books like these, which discuss the different feelings you may have:

Why Can't I Be Happy All The Time? by Mary Atkinson (1997)

Feeling Sad by Helen Frost and Gail Saunders-Smith (2001)

Alexander and the Terrible, Horrible, No Good, Very Bad Day by Judith Viorst (1987)

Wemberly Worried by Kevin Henkes (2000)

On the Web

These websites are also helpful:
www.childanxiety.net
www.kidshealth.org
www.bbc.co.uk/health/kids
www.think-positive.org.uk
www.keepkidshealthy.com
www.youngminds.org.uk

Extra Help

If you would like to talk to someone who doesn't know you, these organisations can help put you in touch with people trained to help:

ChildLine
Studd Street
London
N1 0QW
Tel: 020 7239 1000
Fax: 020 7239 1001

Kidscape
2 Grosvenor Gardens
London
SW1W 0DH
Tel: 020 7730 3300
Fax: 020 7730 7081

The Children's Society
Edward Rudolf House
Margery Street
London WC1X 0JL
Tel: 020 7841 4436
Fax: 020 7841 4500

Index

Photo credits

Abbreviations: t – top, m – middle, b – bottom, r – right, l – left, c – centre. All pictures supplied by Corbis except for 4 both, 7br, 8 both, 11tl, 13t, 17 all, 19tl, 19mr, 23br, 24 all, 27tl, 27bl, 28mrb, 29mlt, 31ml — Select Pictures. 7bl, 28tr — Digital Stock. 11mr — John Foxx Images.

All photographs in this book were posed by models.

The publishers would like to thank them all.